Contents

	How to use this book	
T1.5a	Time problems	3
T1.5b	Quarter past, quarter to	4
T1.5b	15 minutes	5
T1.5c	5 minutes	6–7
T1.5c	Minutes 'past' and 'to'	8
T1.5c	Reading the time	9
T1.5c	am and pm	10
T1.6	Timetables	11–14
M1.3	Which unit?	15
M1.4a	Metres and centimetres	16
M1.4a	Units of length	17
M1.4a	Centimetres	18
M1.4a	Measuring length	19
M1.4b	Grams and kilograms	20
M1.4b	Weight	21
M1.4c	Litres and millilitres	22
M1.4c	Scales	23
M1.4d	Area	24–26
M1.5	Solving problems	27
M1.5	Measurement problems	28
M1.5	Problems	29
M1.5	Measurement problems	30
M1.5	Problems	31

How to use this book

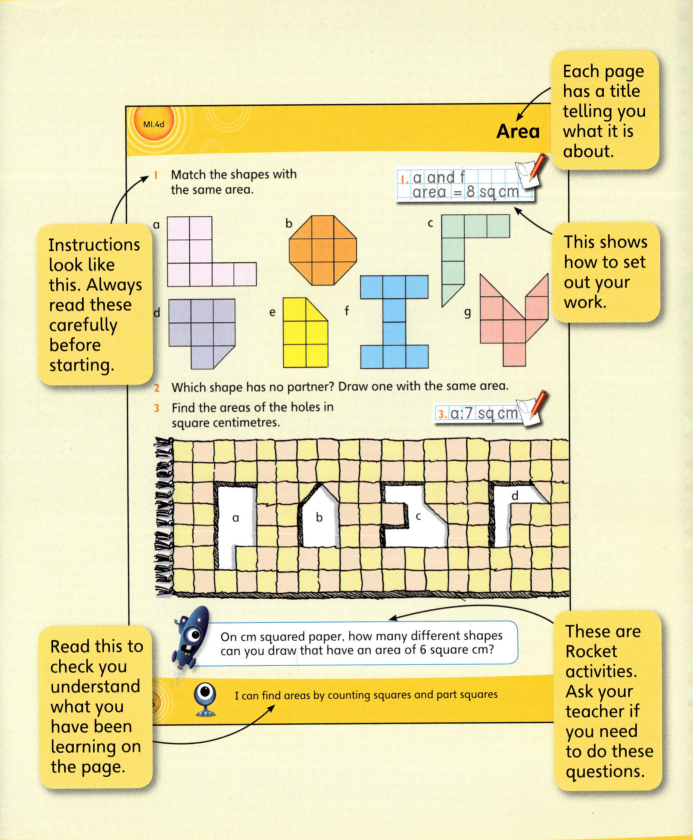

Time problems

Tl.5a

The time is shown on the clock.
Write how long it is until the event.

1  2

3   4

5   6

 Make up problems like these for your partner to do.

Write the time two hours later.

7  8  9  10

I can solve problems about o'clock and half past times

Quarter past, quarter to

The boats have to go back at different times. Write the time which matches each clock.

7. quarter past 2

1  2   3

4   5  6

quarter past 7

quarter past 10

quarter past 4

quarter past 2

quarter to 6

quarter to 9

Write the times, in order, starting at quarter past 2.

Write these times.

7. quarter to 2

7  8  9  10

I can solve problems about quarter to and quarter past times

15 minutes

Monsters take quarter of an hour to eat their meal. These are the starting times. When do they finish?

1. quarter to 3

Monsters sleep for half an hour after their meal. These are the times when they fall asleep. Write what the alarm clock shows when they wake up.

7. 4:30

7	4 o'clock	8	half past 6	9	11 o'clock
10	half past 10	11	quarter past 3	12	quarter past 9
13	quarter to 1	14	half past 8	15	quarter to 7

Monster number 15 wants to sleep until 8 o'clock. The 'snooze' button goes off every 15 minutes. How many times must he hit the button?

I can solve problems about quarters of an hour

5 minutes

Write the number of minutes between each pair of clocks.

1   2   3

4    5   6

7   Sarah leaves home at quarter past 3. She arrives at 3:55. How long is her journey?

8   Pop Special starts at 9:45 and lasts for 25 minutes.
Then Quiz Bang is on for 30 minutes.
What time does Quiz Bang finish?

9   Greg needs to arrive at 8:30. It takes him 40 minutes to have breakfast and walk to school. What time should he start his breakfast?

Write your own story like these!

I can solve problems about time

5 minutes

Write each time:

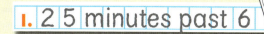
1. 2 5 minutes past 6

1. 15 minutes later
2. 10 minutes earlier
3. 20 minutes later
4. 25 minutes later
5. 35 minutes later
6. 20 minutes earlier

 Write each clock time 100 minutes later.

Write each digital time:

7. 3:25

7. 15 minutes earlier
8. 10 minutes later
9. 25 minutes earlier
10. 20 minutes earlier
11. 15 minutes earlier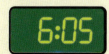
12. 40 minutes later

I can solve problems about time

Minutes 'past' and 'to'

Write the number of minutes past each hour.

Write the number of minutes until the next hour.

Write what time it is right now. Now look at the clocks in the questions. Which one is closest to the time now? Which is furthest away?

9 Write these times in order, between 4 o'clock and 5 o'clock.

10 minutes past 4	19 minutes past 4	11 minutes to 5
quarter to 5	26 minutes to 5	
quarter past 4		20 minutes to 5

  I can solve problems about time

Reading the time

Write the time for each clock using 'past' or 'to'.

1. 27 minutes past 2

1 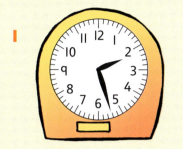 2  3

4  5

Write the digital time to match each clock.

1. 2:27

Write these digital times:

6. 7:55

6 10 minutes later than

7 10 minutes earlier than

8 20 minutes later than

9 20 minutes earlier than

10 25 minutes earlier than

11 15 minutes earlier than

Write the time you wake up. Write the time you go to sleep. How long are you awake? How long are you asleep?

I can read and write the time using minutes

am and pm

Write each time using am or pm.

7 Jon wakes up at 7:45 am. He takes 12 minutes to wash and get dressed, 16 minutes over breakfast, then leaves for school. It takes him 9 minutes to walk to school. What time does he arrive?

Make up a story problem like this for your partner to solve.

Write these times using am or pm.

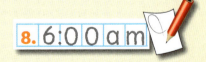

8 six o'clock in the morning

9 quarter to two in the afternoon

10 ten past eight in the evening

11 twenty past midnight

  I can use am and pm times

Timetables

Look at the timetable. Answer the questions.

	Monday	Tuesday	Wednesday	Thursday	Friday
9:00	English	Maths	English	Maths	English
10:45					
11:10	Maths	History / Geography	Maths	Science	Drama
12:20					
1:30	Art	English	RME	English	PE / Music
3:00					

1 What time is Science?   2 On which days do we have Maths?

3 How many times in the week do we have English?

4 Which lessons start at 1:30?   5 Which lessons last $1\frac{3}{4}$ hours?

6 Which are the longest lessons in the day? And the shortest?

7 How long do we spend doing English each week?

Work with a partner to write your own lesson timetable for the week.

3:00 go bowling
5:10 travel to cafe
5:20 start meal
6:45 travel to cinema
7:05 film starts
8:50 film ends

8   How long do we spend bowling?
9   Which part of the day takes longest?
10 How long do we spend travelling?
11 Which takes longer, the meal or the film?

 I can interpret timetables

Timetables

1. Look at these facts. Draw up a timetable.

Rocket leaves Moon
7:15 am
9:00 am
3:00 pm
6:00 pm

Rocket arrives at Mars
11:00 am
12:20 pm
7:00 pm
12:00 midnight

Rocket arrives at Jupiter
1:00 pm
3:40 pm
10:00 pm
7:25 am

2. Which is the quickest rocket to Mars?
3. What time do I reach Mars if I leave the Moon at 3:00 pm?
4. What is the latest time I can leave Mars to get to Jupiter?
5. Which is the slowest rocket to Jupiter?

6. Look at this timetable. Choose four journeys. Write how long each journey takes.

LONDON ▶ ALL DESTINATIONS   Monday to Saturday

Notes	London	Ashford	Calais	Lille	Brussels	Paris	Train
1	05:34	06:27				09:23	9078
1	06:10	06:59		08:56	09:37		9106
2	06:27	07:20		09:18	10:01		9108
	06:34	07:24	08:56			10:23	9002
1	07:09	07:59		09:56		10:59	9004
2	07:39	08:29				11:23	9006
	07:43				10:58		9112

I can interpret timetables

Timetables

1. Copy the timetable and fill in the gaps.

Tour timetable

Entrance	Zebras	Monkeys	Lions	Penguins
9:30	9:40	9:50	10:00	10:10
10:20	10:30			
12:15		12:35		
2:45			3:15	
4:05	4:15			

2. Draw up a timetable for the wardens using the information below.

We feed the tigers for an hour at 7:00 am and at 3:00 pm.

We clean out the tigers after we have fed them.

We give the baby tiger its vitamins at 10:00 am and at 5:00 pm.

It takes an hour to clean out the tigers.

It takes half an hour to provide fresh straw.

We provide fresh straw at 1:00 pm.

We shut the tigers in their house at 6:00 pm.

I can interpret timetables

Timetables

Look at the timetable. Answer the children's questions.

Belfast	Coleraine	Derry
8:40 am	9:30 am	11:50 am
11:40 am	12:30 pm	2:50 pm
1:30 pm	2:30 pm	5:00 pm

1. What time do we leave Belfast to get to Derry at 5:00 pm?
2. Which train is slowest from Coleraine to Derry?
3. How long will it take to get from Belfast to Coleraine if I take the 1:30 pm train?
4. How long will it take to get from Coleraine to Derry on the 9:30 am train?
5. Which is the slowest train from Belfast to Coleraine?
6. How long will it take from Belfast to Derry on the 1:30 pm train?

The railway from Coleraine to Derry is being mended so all the journeys take an extra 10 minutes. What are the new times the trains arrive at Derry?

7. The children are going home tomorrow. They have worked out a timetable to make sure they catch the train. Work out how long they have for each activity.

7:15	start getting up
7:35	start eating breakfast
7:55	start cleaning teeth
8:00	start packing bags
8:20	start walking to station
9:00	get on train

Work with a partner to write a timetable for your normal school morning.

I can interpret timetables

Which unit?

Write which unit of measurement you would use for each answer.

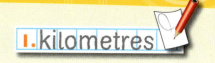

1. kilometres

| millimetres | centimetres | metres | kilometres |
| grams | kilograms | millilitres | litres |

1 How far is it to fly from Edinburgh to Paris?

2 How long is a millipede?

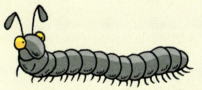

3 How heavy is a conker?

4 How much water is in a paddling pool?

5 What is the width of a football pitch?

6 How long is an ant?

7 How much pop is in a can of fizzy drink?

8 How heavy is a cow?

Make up a question like this for your partner to answer.

I can suggest a sensible unit to use

Metres and centimetres

1. Write which animals are taller than 1 metre.
2. Write which animals are shorter than 1 metre.

3. Write 3 animals which are longer than 10 centimetres.
4. Write 3 animals which are shorter than 10 centimetres.

Think of 10 animals and write them down. Put them in order of length.

I can talk about a metre and 10 centimetres.

Units of length

Write which unit of length is best to use each time.

| millimetres | centimetres | metres | kilometres |

1 the length of a lorry

2 the width of a butterfly

3 the length of a rabbit

4 the height of a ferris wheel

5 the length of a train journey

6 the depth of a jug

7 the thickness of a coin

8 the height of a giraffe

Now make up two problems like these for your partner to do.

I can choose a sensible unit of length

Centimetres

Write the length of each caterpillar in centimetres.

1. 5 cm

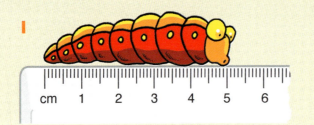

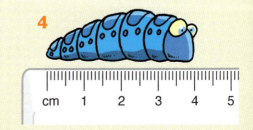

Estimate each pencil's length in centimetres.
Then use a ruler to measure it.

5. Estimate: 6 cm
   Length: 7 cm

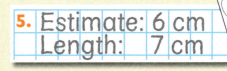

Draw a wiggly line more than 15 cm long.

I can estimate and measure using centimetres

Measuring length

You will need some measuring equipment and:

a shoe  a jumper

a T-shirt 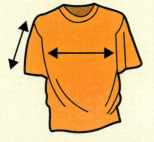 a trainer

Measure:

1. the length of the shoe
2. the width of the shoe
3. the height of the shoe
4. the length of the jumper's sleeve
5. the width of the jumper's chest
6. the length of the T-shirt's sleeve
7. the width of the T-shirt's chest
8. the length of the trainer
9. the height of the trainer

1. the length of the shoe is …. cm

Which measurements did you find hard to do? Explain why they were hard.

I can use equipment to measure length

Grams and kilograms

Here are the weights of some items in a shop.

1 kg   50 g   35 g

Use the weight of the flour, beans and crisps to help you estimate the weights of these things.

1   2    3    4 

1   2   3   4

5   6   7   8

Write how many of each will weigh 1 kilogram.

9   10   11

100 g   500 g   200 g

12   13   14

50 g   10 g   250 g

 I can estimate using grams and kilograms

Weight

Match each pet with the correct scale.

1
2 kg 900 g

2
2 kg 400 g

3
4 kg 400 g

4
700 g

5
9 kg 600 g

6
1 kg 300 g

7
6 kg 800 g

8
4 kg 600 g

9
2 kg 300 g

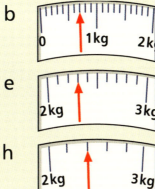
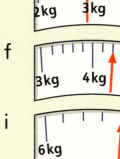

Write the weight of each pet in grams, for example 2900 g.

I can read scales

Litres and millilitres

Are these 'more than', 'less than' or 'equal to' 1 litre?

1. less

1   800 ml

2   1200 ml

3   1000 ml

4   200 ml

5   500 ml

6   250 ml

Write how much more or less than 1 litre each time.

7   How many of container 4 do you need to make 1 litre?
8   How many of container 5 do you need to make 1 litre?
9   How many of container 6 do you need to make 1 litre?

Write the number of millilitres.

10. 1000 ml

10   1 l

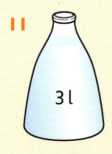
11   3 l

12   5 l

13   ½ l

I can say how litres and millilitres are related

Scales

How much water in each?
Write the answer in millilitres.

1. 800 ml

1 2 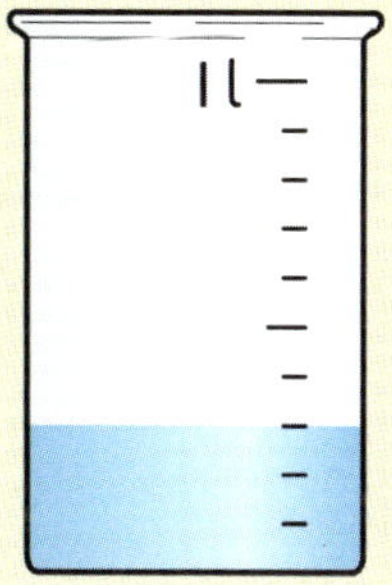 3 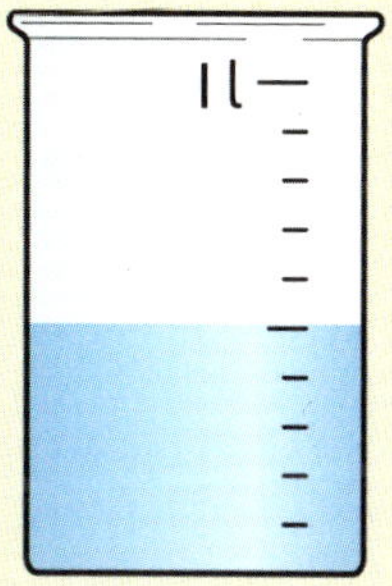 4

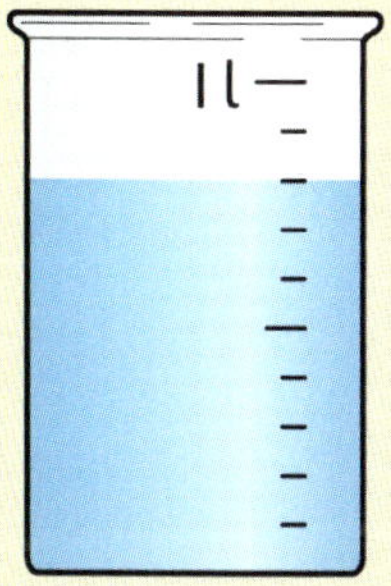

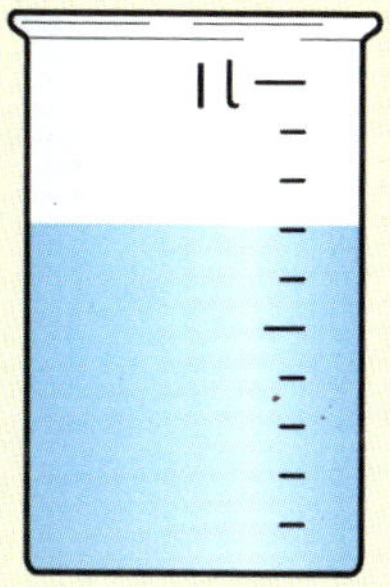

5  6 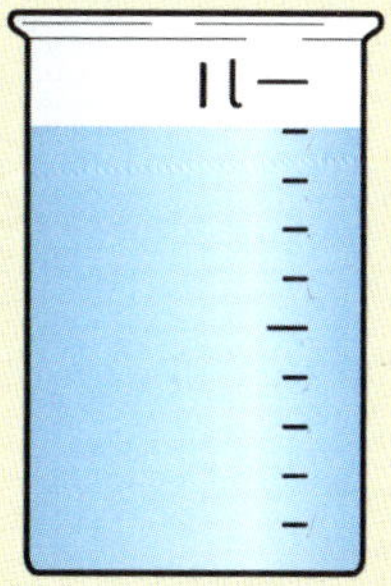 7 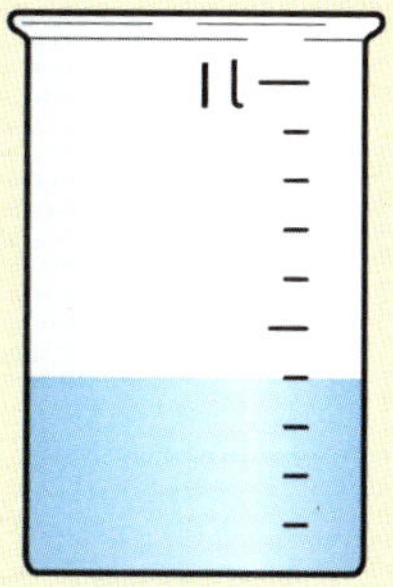 8

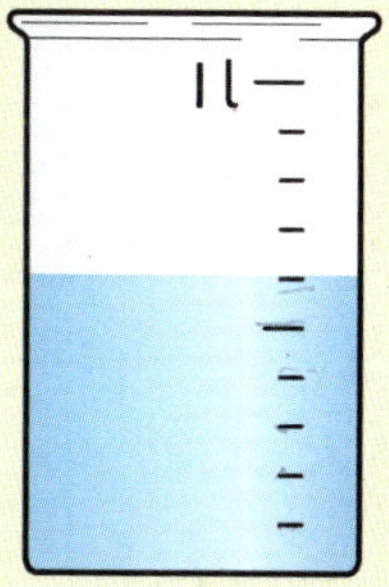

9 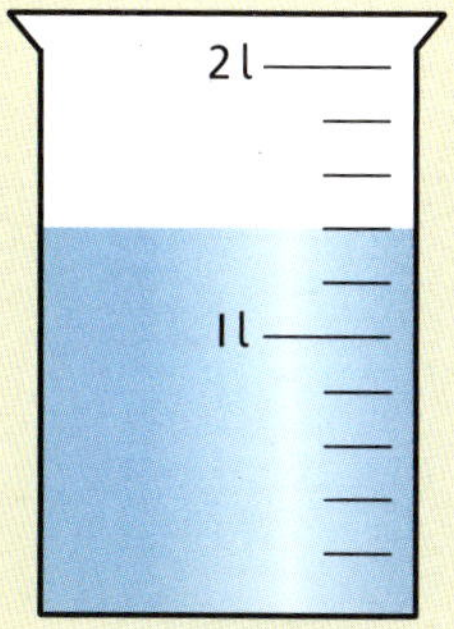 10 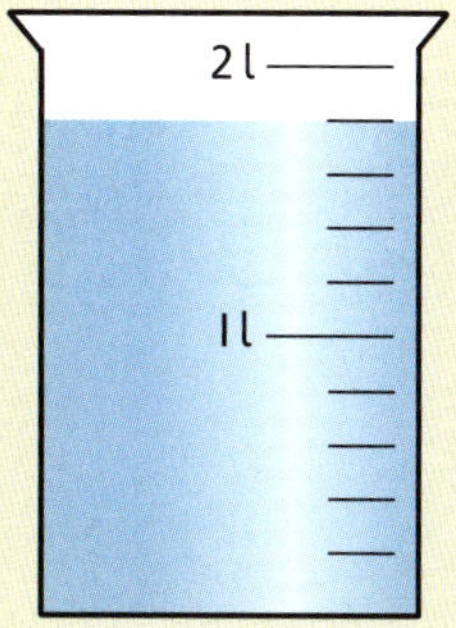 11 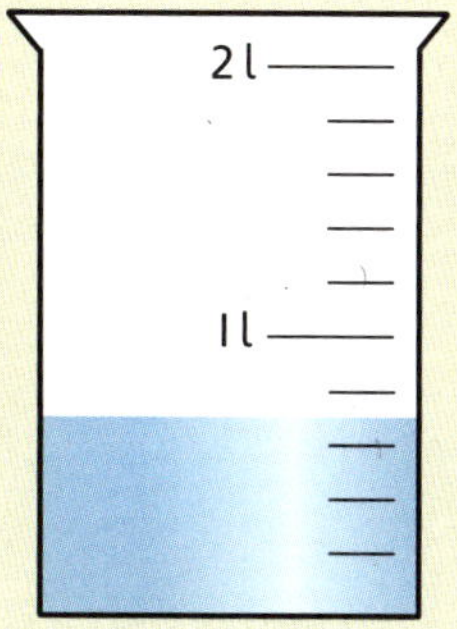 12

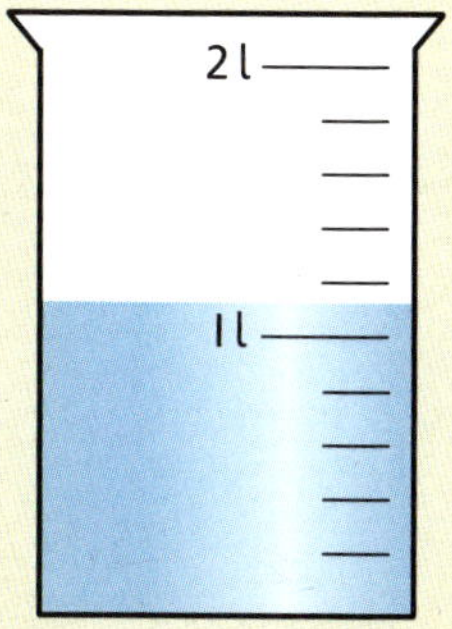

Find a pair of these containers that together hold 2 litres. How many different pairs can you find?

I can read scales

Area

Write the area of each shape in squares.

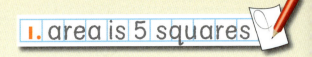

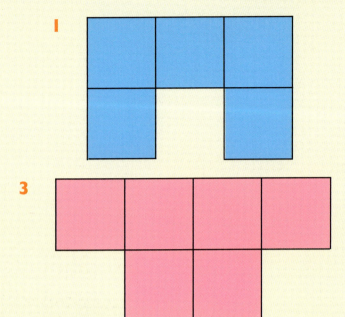

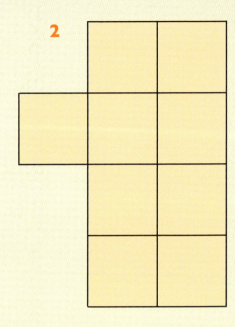

Look at Question 1. What other ways can you find to arrange 5 squares?

Write the area of tiles on each floor.

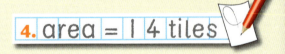

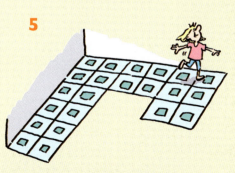

7 Draw a room with 20 tiles on the floor.

I can find areas by counting squares

Area

Write the area of each stain. Only count part squares if they are half a square or more.

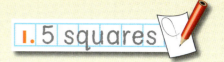

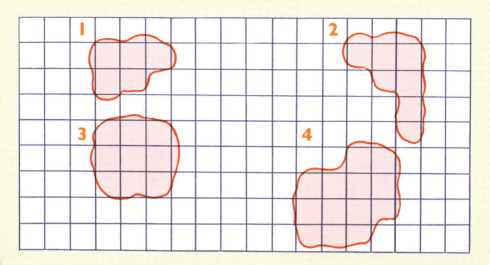

With a partner, each draw round your hand on centimetre squared paper. What is the area of your hand in squares?

Find the area of each shape.

11 For Questions 5 to 10, draw another shape that has the same area.

I can find areas by counting squares and part squares

Area

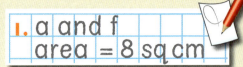

1. Match the shapes with the same area.

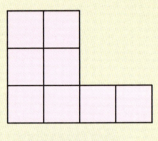

1. a and f
area = 8 sq cm

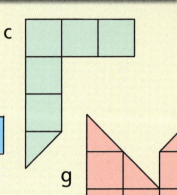

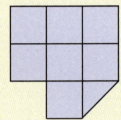

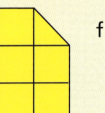

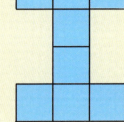

2. Which shape has no partner? Draw one with the same area.
3. Find the areas of the holes in square centimetres.

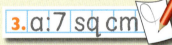

3. a: 7 sq cm

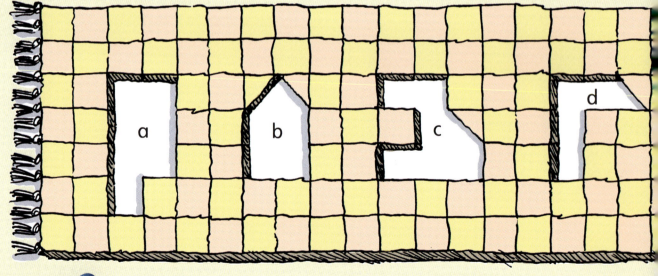

On cm squared paper, how many different shapes can you draw that have an area of 6 square cm?

I can find areas by counting squares and part squares

Solving problems

George
1m 41cm

Yuko
1m 15cm

Jane
85cm

Emma
1m 25cm

Will
91cm

How much taller is:

1 Will than Jane
2 Emma than Will
3 Emma than Yuko
4 George than Yuko
5 Emma than Jane
6 George than Will

Find out your own height.

What is the difference in height between you and:

7 Jane
8 George
9 Will
10 Yuko

I can solve problems about length

Measurement problems

Which of these pieces of equipment would you use to answer each question?

ruler   scales   measuring jug   tape measure   metre stick

1 How wide is a CD?

2 How thin is a matchstick?

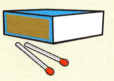

3 How much water does a water bottle hold?

4 How heavy is a football?

5 How heavy is a book?

6 What is the capacity of a juice carton?

7 What is your waist measurement?

8 How long is your classroom?

 Which unit of measurement would you use for each answer?

 I can solve measurement problems

Problems

True or false?

1. Half a litre is the same as 500 ml.

2. Five cans, each holding 350 ml, is more than one bottle holding 1½ litres.

3. If I drink 300 ml of orange juice a day, two 1 litre packs will last me for a week.

4. Two hundred 5 ml spoonfuls will fill a litre jug.

Solve these problems.

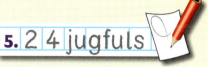

5. A jug holds 250 ml of water. How many jugfuls do I need to fill a sink which holds 6 litres?

6. A recipe needs 1½ litres of chicken stock. A cup holds 150 ml of stock. How many cupfuls of stock are needed for the recipe?

7. A can holds 300 ml of fizzy drink. Gary bought a pack of 12 cans. How much fizzy drink does he have?

8. A teaspoon holds 5 ml. How many teaspoons of medicine are there in a ½ litre bottle?

9. Simret took 250 ml of orange juice to a picnic. She drank half of it at lunchtime, then drank another 65 ml in the afternoon. How much was left in the carton?

10. A tin holds 450 ml of soup. Bob needs to make enough soup so six people can have 300 ml each. How many tins does he need?

Make up your own story using litres and millilitres.

I can solve problems about capacity

Measurement problems

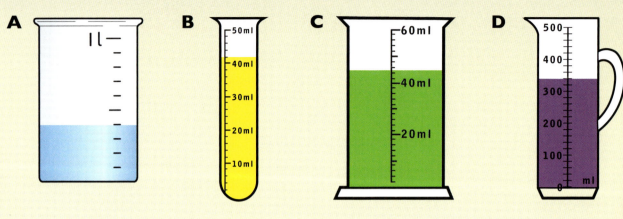

1. A = 400 ml

1. Write the amounts of magic potion in each container.

2. How much more potion does container C have than container B?

3. If the wizard combines all the potions, how much liquid will she have?

4. The wizard uses 250 ml of potion from container D. How much is left?

5. The wizard adds 5 ml of potion to container C. How much has she now?

6. The wizard pours the contents of containers A and B into a clean cauldron. How much liquid is in her cauldron now? How much water must she add to make it up to 1 litre?

Write a measurement problem of your own for your partner to solve.

I can solve measurement problems

Problems

1. A plum weighs 50 g. If I buy 1 kg of plums, how many plums will I have?

2. Each melon weighs 500 grams. What is the weight in kilograms of 10 melons?

3. Sarita bought a 5 kg bag of potatoes. For each meal she cooks 400 g of them. What weight of potatoes is left after 10 meals have been eaten?

4. The contents of a tin of tomatoes weigh 250 g. A recipe requires 2 kg of tomatoes. How many tins are needed?

True or false?

5. Ten 100 g weights weigh 1 kilogram.

6. Two and a half kilograms is heavier than six 500 g weights.

7. If one tomato weighs 40 grams, a kilogram of tomatoes contains 22 tomatoes.

8. 1 kilogram of potatoes is heavier than 1 kilogram of feathers.

$\frac{1}{2}$ kg = 500 grams

Investigate other fractions of kilograms.

I can solve measurement problems

Author Team: Lynda Keith, Hilary Koll and Steve Mills
Consultant: Siobhán O'Doherty

Published by Pearson Education Limited, a company incorporated in England and Wales, having its registered office at Edinburgh Gate, Harlow, Essex, CM20 2JE. Registered company number: 872828

www.pearsonschools.co.uk

Text © Pearson Education Limited 2012

First published 2012

15 14 13 12
10 9 8 7 6 5 4 3 2 1

British Library Cataloguing in Publication Data
A catalogue record for this book is available from the British Library

ISBN 978 0 435 07732 7

Copyright notice
All rights reserved. No part of this publication may be reproduced in any form or by any means (including photocopying or storing it in any medium by electronic means and whether or not transiently or incidentally to some other use of this publication) without the written permission of the copyright owner, except in accordance with the provisions of the Copyright, Designs and Patents Act 1988 or under the terms of a licence issued by the Copyright Licensing Agency, Saffron House, 6–10 Kirby Street, London EC1N 8TS (www.cla.co.uk). Applications for the copyright owner's written permission should be addressed to the publisher.

Typeset by Debbie Oatley @ room9design and revised by Mike Brain Graphic Design Limited, Oxford
Illustrations © Harcourt Education Limited 2006–2007, Pearson Education Limited 2011
Illustrated by Piers Baker, Matt Buckley, Seb Burnett, Andy Hammond, John Haslam, Andrew Hennessey, Nigel Kitching, Debbie Oatley, Jim Peacock, Mark Ruffle, Anthony Rule, Eric Smith, Gary Swift, Annabel Tempest, Dave Williams, Chris Winn
Cover design by Pearson Education Limited
Cover illustration by Volker Beisler © Pearson Education Limited
Printed in the UK by Scotprint

Acknowledgements
The Publishers would like to thank the following for their help and advice:
Liam Monaghan
Hilary Keane
Stephen Walls

Every effort has been made to contact copyright holders of material reproduced in this book.
Any omissions will be rectified in subsequent printings if notice is given to the publishers.